The Next Ancient World

The

Next Ancient World

World

Jennifer Michael Hecht

TUPELO PRESS

Dorset, Vermont

The Next Ancient World
Copyright © 2001 Jennifer Michael Hecht

ISBN 0-9710310-0-2
Printed in Canada

Library of Congress Control Number: 2001132520

Second paperback edition, 2003.

Cover and book design by
William Kuch, WK Graphic Design

Tupelo Press
PO Box 539, Dorset, Vermont 05251
802.366.8185 • Fax 802.362.1883
editor@tupelopress.org • web www.tupelopress.org

For John

Acknowledgments

THE PARTISAN REVIEW: *History, Gods and Animals*

THE SOUTHERN REVIEW: *The Army Medical Museum of My Heart*

THE GETTYSBURG REVIEW: *Send in the Swans, At Some Point Out, The Innocent*

QUARTERLY WEST: *Crossing*

POETRY: *Rapture*

SALMAGUNDI: *So You're A Little Mentally Ill*

THE MISSOURI REVIEW: *How to Go Home, Totem and Taboo, Swamp Thing, A Victorian Construction, Trotsky's Hand*

THE ANTIOCH REVIEW: *September*

NERVE: *Naked*

CONFRONTATION: *Tiger Story*

DELMAR: *Two at a Time, Felonies*

THE DENVER QUARTERLY: *Telling the Future*

THE PRAIRIE SCHOONER: *Villanelle If You Want to Be a Bad-Ass, Waiting to Happen*

RIVER CITY: *Sailing with Virgins*

JUDAISM: *Exodus*

September has been reprinted in THE BEST AMERICAN POETRY 1999, Robert Bly and David Lehman, eds. (Scribners, 1999).

The Innocent has also appeared in POETRY DAILY, February 9, 2000.

Sailing with Virgins has been nominated for a Pushcart Prize, 2001.

Table of Contents

Prologue

My first real project was a study of the deathbed gestures
of nine famous failures.

Then I wrote the book on one successful woman and her seven hazy
memories of regret.

Next came a novel about a woman who had certain habits.

She wore nail polish in the winter to keep her nails warm
and hated people who wore it in the summer.
For her there were a whole lot of things that were sacrilege.
No fish in the kitchen, no shoes after noon.

She had taboos up the kazoo.
Then, at some point, I became interested in the passage of time
and stopped work on the novel.
Now all spring the woman with the habits rattles around my head, extant,
worrying a cotton ball, trying to get the last bit of red paint off her left
thumbnail like goddamn Lady Macbeth.

My latest project is to sketch several careful descriptions for the benefit
of the next ancient world: a sort of advice book, so that they will
understand that civilization has phases, even phases about believing
in phases, and ideas about gods, and the anthropomorphizing of animals,
and about how the idea of progress
gets in the way of certain things while making other things possible,
and about how the idea of the fall from grace also allows
a number of transactions but blocks others.

They should know, this time, how to approach the fact that as history
unfolds, some people will describe the world as a struggle between good
and evil and other people will insist upon caprice.
This is the sort of advice I'm talking about.

Some indication about the real and unreal continuity of ideas across
history; the real and unreal continuity of the self over time.
How worlds reprise; how my wounded heart came
to revive. Because the next ancient world
is likely to be as curious as the last one was
and while information about the last one seems
to be accruing over time as we gather shards of data out of the alluvial
fields, we also have to admit that the important parts are the parts
that we remember in the lower parts of our bodies,
the way the seat of your pants knows things about the acropolis.

We are forgetting, like dye dissipating in a glass of ocean water,
and that is why I feel it would be a good idea to get down some precise
observations, memories as well as memorials, and not just
to amuse our friends but to capture what it is that I know about
what happened here; since
in the long run,
a few well-placed words go a great deal farther than crop circles
in our factual and fictional quest for direction.
A map is only as good as its key. As is a lock.

So take this in the spirit in which it was written: as a lock of a lover's
hair. As a skeleton key to the heart of the matter.

The ventricles, the chambers, the pulse. A collection of auguries. Grist
for a mill that is yet to be built. Our hard-worn highways will slip
from heavy usefulness into the mythos of the next ancient world.
The signs are all there, bear right, approaching toll, end construction. Right
lane must turn right. Left lane must careen into the distance carrying our
best intentions like mismatched baggage and sounding,
endlessly, its baleful horn,
as the universe expands into the night.

The Innocent

The knack to almost everything is merely to commit to it, utterly,
and yet we fail, constantly. Is this commitment, this certainty of intention,
what innocence was?
Let us commit to the proposition: Innocence is certainty.

You're not sure you believe me.

You're innocent when you are born.
You accrue guiltiness. Like lichen? You fade to guilt, like evolution,
or topographical gradation.
You make decisions.

Until you are proven guilty, you may keep your innocence. Like a pet.
Even before you have committed the crime (if I had a gun, I'd kill him)
letters are being sent out to possible jurors.
It's just the way the system works; they have to keep
ahead of things. If you decide not to do it,
they will use the jurors for someone else.
Among the people presently considering a crime,
some of them will decide to do it.
On the street outside your window the men and women
who might judge you are presently walking by.

You are still innocent.
Now is your chance to court their affections.
Get out there. Now is the time to get in touch
with the opinions and predilections of your peers.
In the end, it is their decision. Win them over.
Consider your life as a campaign
for the eventual trial. You do not know
what you might do at the height of some passion.
Prepare now.

You are innocent in prayer.
As an exercise, to renew your faith in the legal system,
reply by saying: *According to the Constitution,*
we each have at least twelve peers
when next a friend asks, smoothing her hips,
if there's anyone left out there.

Discretion is nine-tenths of innocence. The tenth tenth
is having not committed the crime.
When next a friend asks you if you would help dispatch
the body of her lover, if it came to that, say,
while leaning back in a lawn chair, drinking something
cold as the condensation douses your hand almost
sexually, almost violently:
It is not his fault that he is close-minded
and self-aggrandizing, nor is it his mother's fault,
though she taught him to do it,
it isn't his mother's father's fault,
though his absences spoke,
it isn't even the great-grandfather's fault,
though his meekness wore down the thatch in his cane chair,
or even the great-great-grandmother's fault,
though she drank potato wine at sunrise.
It is her mother's fault.
Your lover's great-great-great-grandmother.
She had free will and chose to use it for evil.
She has ruined your life.

Someone has ruined your innocent life.
Some gesture of your mother,
tapping her lip with her finger; some way your father
looked from his school-day etchings marked
full of promise and back at you;
or something handed down in your family, perhaps
an inability to apologize
or a general distrust, has somehow hamstrung
what you were trying to get done.

It's no secret, nowadays, that there are no heroes
and there is no blame. You may still find love.
It's all right. Give me the gun.

You're innocent when you chew. You are innocent
when your pants are around your ankles, and you stare directly
at the sun, and children mock you. They don't know
what is in store for them; what loneliness,
what terrible conviction, what commitment
to what unbearable truth.
Don't be sorry, just tell me the truth.
What did you do?

It is exhausting watching you claim your innocence,
aping emptiness.
Have you even considered the possibility that you did
do it? Or (more to the point) that it was done to you?
Either way you are not innocent. You are aware.
We will make no decisions about love today
and nobility will go undefined.

These convictions are not binding.
We have lost our knack for law.

Two at a Time

Remember the first house you can remember,
how the stairway hung from nowhere,
unconnected to the floor from which you were
bounding away and floating free from the landing
to which you were flinging yourself, the torque of your perfect legs
projecting you towards your room or the room
you shared; what if you knew now
what went through your mind, not all the time
of your childhood, but just then,
                              just a script
of your mind while on those stairs, each time, what thoughts
would therein be recorded beyond a steady refrain of
two-at-a-time, two-at-a-time? What will you wonder
thirty years from now when all of this has the same unconnectedness,
when the office where you work will hang
in the air of memory without hinges,
without crosswalks, what litany of concern, what
delicate structure of related thoughts
will you wish you could recall, could reassemble,
                              thirty years from now,
when all the cars today on Broadway
are vintage cars, and we, the populace of the present,
glow out our individual and collective ignorance
of some particular future event, the innocence of which
makes us shimmer when photographed as if, if you
could only speak to us, we could grant you some wish,
and whisper what it was to live before.

Crossing

More importantly, to what body part
is Juliet reducible
if the name Romeo is neither hand,
nor foot, nor heart? Perhaps she is Romeo.
It is essentially a matter of balconies, then?
Perhaps a classifying system might be drawn up:
bare marble, ivy-entwined, high up
with a light inside it, covered in toads,
affixed with star-crossed lovers, freshly painted,
seen from far away, overlooking Central Park,
sticky, and so forth. Just a way
to reveal the gender of the building
and perhaps its attitude towards penetration
("the orchard walls are high and hard
to climb!").

While we can not fix the story to a particular life,
we can see that it lives.

It is difficult to know if we're invited into it.
The castle's thighs are slightly parted,
its moat de-crocked, its embankments
trimmed with rope. And yet the bridge
is up. Finally, the whole thing has to be left
unclear, un-deciphered. Patience,
it may yet rain. Keep dancing. For my part, what I protest
to be (what I intend to present) loses a great deal
in translation and the loss seems
unrecoverable, as if extending myself
out of myself, if only enough to be seen
by human eyes, is enough to step out
into nothingness and fall. Consider the echo
between unspeakables. It is the sound of the lost
and found. This is where to go if you are missing
something. There is a lot of room between unspeakable rituals, unspeakable
words, and unspeakable sex.
Go look. Your gold watch might be in there.

Crossing into Brando is astonishing.
Put on a black cap and white t-shirt,
and dangle a pencil from your lips like
a cigarette. Sit backwards on a kitchen chair.
What is the position of the drawbridge now?

And are we all invited?

In this wash of messages, of hypnotic
suggestions, it is impossible to know
to which ones you have responded.
You may be crowing like a rooster
every twenty minutes and buying lousy,
overpriced, brand names. If you were,
you wouldn't notice it. Yet the people
around you are wrong to think they know
the ways in which you have been
hypnotized. For all they know,
you actually are a rooster. For all they know,
you are the finest rooster that has ever lived.
For all you know,
my rain dance brings the rain.

Everyone's eyes shut off
and you disappear. Or, you decide
you don't exist and as a result, no one
can see you anymore. I'm not sure
which it is. Still, if you shift,
and shift again, you will eventually
reappear—though it will be to a different
faculty of the population. It's a matter of hide
and go seek. A matter of lost and found.
And wherever you find yourself, friends,
there you are. Take it from me, Romeo, you're
a hell of a rooster. Every time it rains, it rains.
Watch me now.

Send in the Swans

I

Summer streets and the ring
sent back. Like my hand might
float away, it felt at first. Now, nothing.
Just a stubborn taste of skin when I
look around and there is Leda on every
street corner. Everywhere, unknowing.
She seems to think that she's the swan.
You should have seen my face as I figured it out.

II

I'm the swan.
After the rain, the grass still complains of dryness.
It takes predators longer, is what I discovered.
Sadists come and go like food allergies.
But predators need several lives
to find their nature and several more
to isolate their style.

No one knew anything
until I talked in my sleep.
I only mentioned a few nouns,
but the damage was done.

Now it makes sense. About me. All along the one that.
Scared me the most. Was what I was (and now I remember
that I always knew. People had always mentioned they could
hear my black wings in the air just beyond me) and I had
always known about the length of my neck
and the pride of my breast.

It was worth it. Traveling these legends.
My life sang to its chains.
At the end of your life, it is certain that you stretched out your tongue just
the right number of times.

But until then, you can not be so certain.
There are so many good ideas
and yet we get into a lot of repetition.
In literature as well as hip to hip: the milkweed
repeats. So do the iron bars.
So do the women in white.
So does the gun in gun-corner awaiting gun-master.

And I'm the swan. Once I let it in, it took me over.

Once upon a time, Zeus came down
from Mount Olympus with a stiff beak and a stiffer countenance,
swanishly, and saw a round-hipped, pale-milk with red hair
swept around her neck and sequined clothes,
and the darkness of a diamond shadow between
her uppermost thighs,
leaning, between acts, against a circus tent rope,
taut with holding up the big top,
and Zeus went all swan to get her.

Just after, he drank water from the wrong stream
and lost his memory: forgot he was Zeus.
Saw in reflection his self and found himself
so lovely that he almost turned to stone.
Waited for a god to fall in love.

I wish I could have been there when he snapped
out of it and realized what he was and who.
I bet he got the lipstick off his beak in a hurry.

Catholicism seems like a good idea sometimes. Especially
for the captain of my ship. I suspect perversion in him; I want him

to confess my sins to an Irish girl with her skirt caught hypnotically
in her sock.

A monster knows what it is. That's generally why it destroys the city.

I wish I could proceed from anything like that. Anything with only
two hands. Anything with only one head on its shoulder. And yet, I liked
both of the kisses that got planted on me today.
And that is not a small matter, friends,
and when I walk around
from now on, mind, I am not walking.

The first bird ever,
leaned over to the other,
and said: It is a wonder
I can fly, given the weight of my wings.

Isn't it rich? Are we a pair? You here
at last on the ground,
me in mid-air.

Leda, I am almost at my end.

Please
I'm quiet now,
show me.

A Victorian Construction

It's a complicated question starting from one central point and radiating.
It starts from the smell of flesh

and that smell, once conjured, proceeds to the desire to taste
the remembered scent. Someone once said something

to each of us. To me he described an auburn swish of satin hair, achingly
soft, gathering in a tiny swirl at his lost

lover's tailbone. What must he or she have said to you to have incited
such desire for me? There was the fur

on the face of the girl in French class, in high school,
a mild fascination at the time, grown to a cult

of blond wisps edged out along the memory
of her parchment cheek. Then on through years on wisps

we arrive at my personal comprehension of the gentleman
stalking Victorian London

for a touch; at home, his wife, otherwise reviled of flesh, strokes
her own where it joins her pinned up hair

fascinated by the upsweep of its particulate fluidity, its soft redness
blushing with silent revelation. The mirror,

the ivory brush, the warmth of the room shifting with her
proximity to, or distance from, the caged fire

and the latticed window. Out there, working-class girls
know everything. Two shop girls, getting off at nine,

wearing each other's clothes, see him. The four of them
(two young girls, one wife, one husband) move with caution

in the world; each of them in desperate haste, disguised.
Each of them, fearing, above all else, the shame

of prostitution, and all monitor their behavior for a sign
of trade. Trade is everywhere. Yet each one avoids

that part of trade that scares them most. It is not
the easiest approach they could have taken and anxiety

in this regard joins each to all. On each person's body something
somewhere has been the object of some secret

conversation. The memory of a wisp of hair, shared, plants the memory
of desire into a second mind which goes out

looking for it, certain that he or she has already seen it somewhere
(French class. High school.) and wanted it.

And wept like winter rain: almost cold enough to be snow, and yet,
it is rain. Almost wanting nothing. And yet.

And yet this is the latticework through which bedroom light
arranges a strangely human pattern on the patio slate.

Such comprehension as the world allows is then synaptic;
the leaps of memory are patterns of desire

and from one's own desire one must step out, out in all directions, to
belief about the desire of others and why

they do those things and why they are sometimes to be seen on their
knees and elsewhere, also, they will

willingly be ruined, their bodies overcome with nostalgia, their fingers
tracing a swirl of hair that they saw once,

later heard about, and then searched for, and found.
No law or shame could force it free again. This tiny,

auburn swirl of trade, this body lost in latticework,
this certainty of marvelous desire.

Carnal Knowledge

This is years ago, love sitting on my couch.
Him, suddenly awake saying, Please Ann-Margret,
Please Ann-Margret, as I clicked by her
on my way up the scale of channels.
We dipped back and watched her for a while, all that red hair, the lippy,
opening bud of a face.
These are the things one keeps, after all, little spells
that lose all connection to their source.
When all seems lost and musters up a prayer
from somewhere, when no knee, but something entrailish
and hidden seeks to bend, then it comes
to my head, Please, Ann-Margret. Please, Ann-Margret.
As if Ann-Margret, well, you understand.
It's a matter of liturgy.

If you build a town, keep the gates narrow
so the buffalo hooves of love-of-life
can not stampede. Let, instead, one solitary
pair of beasts wander through the streets
now and again, on holidays and feasts,
sweating and hard-breathing with the glory.

Alone in cool clean sheets.
Home. Silent and eating
white rice. Alone
on the couch with short
clean hair. My books. Silent,
with short cotton socks.
Alone in the clean ease of winter.

Please, Ann-Margret, walking in the streets at dawn,
cold air condensing your hot breath,
the town still asleep, and in the square,
by the church, two enormous beasts
silhouette their black and humpèd bodies
against the wall of stone.
These premonitions tend to tell me more

about the past than of the future. Full hands,
full belly, full mouth.
I remember hunger and fulfilling. I remember anger
and its harrowing relief. A winnowing of needs
and then a feeding frenzy. A desert.
A forest of rain.
Please, Annmargret, I'm still not ready to go back again.
But the steam, the way it rises from their bodies in the cold.

The way they find each other's hot, gigantic faces
and stroke their heavy hooves against the cobbled stone.
The way their meat surrounds their bones.
Please, Annmargret. Home.

The Army Medical Museum of My Heart

Is a two-headed baby a poem about awkwardness and love
and feeling tired? Well, yes. Both look in several
directions at once, both haunt and fade. Both recall
some primordial ocean panoply. I would not feel strange.

I'm not the only one who twitches to lift her out of her
formaldehyde, from where her auburn under-feathers
of hair swoon around her gentle, addled heads,
and hold her on my belly nursing both her tiny mouths.

In scientific glass, there she floats, hands open,
safe from our desire, cradled among the anatomically improbable,
the elephantiasis leg in a tank, the mock-up of President McKinley's
assassinated frame (crank to bleed).

It feels shameful, but it is no shame to dream.

Naked

The reason you so often in literature have a naked woman
walk out of her house that way, usually older, in her front garden
or on the sidewalk, oblivious, is because of exactly how I feel right now.

You tend to hear about how it felt to come upon such a mythical beast,
the naked woman on the street, the naked man in a tree, and that makes
sense because it is wonderful to take the naked woman by the hand

And know that you will remember that moment for the rest of your life
because of what it means, the desperation, the cataclysm of what it takes
to leave your house naked or to take off your clothes in the tree.

It feels good to get the naked man to come down from there by a series
of gentle commands and take him by the elbow or her by the hand and
lead him to his home like you would care for a bird or a human heart.

Still if you want instead, for once, to hear about how the person came to be
standing there, naked, outside, you should talk to me right now, quickly,
before I forget the details of this way that I feel. I feel like walking out.

Felonies

Loneliness is criminal, but the law
spits and looks the other way.
Every night, hooligans break into my apartment,
kick the phone until it rings, and disappear
before I can arrive; shaken, unwell, and in
disrepair. How else can I explain all of those bells?

It couldn't possibly be you, out there
in night's phone booth, calling and falling away.
The world is full of such wonderful alibis. You and I
are as wise as only silent, tired things can be,
no more assailed by lust or filibust or the turning
of your interminable key.

I insist: We are past all harm. How else
can I explain, through such adversity,
the persistence of all our wild virginities?
Everything is air-tight. All of my lies
are true. I answer the phone in the middle
of the night: it is you again, it is always you.

First Avenue

I live above a laundromat and over from a vet so all day long and some
of the night strangers bring, seemingly to me, their clothing and their
pets: ill, filthy and then, leaving, well and clean.

Of course, it makes me feel powerful, like Prospero, like the tempest
of their lives and its abetting is all actually in my control. From my
fire-escape, friends of mine watch brightly-colored laundry sacks hoisted
on shoulders, and cats in plastic boxes peering through grid windows.
They compliment my vantage point like visiting monarchs, comparing it
internally with their own stores, and foot traffic, and building tops.

And then one morning I can't remember what is the good of it all.
Some part of my body hurts and then all parts of my body start to hurt,
in sympathy. I take out the garbage but it doesn't work, I can't get
the house clean. I keep thinking about how the first time I saw
a Venetian blind cleaner advertised, which is really just a serrated piece
of sponge on a stick, I thought of a visually impaired domestic
from Venice and figured she must have left there to avoid drowning.

So I am considering going to the vet. Just marching in there and saying,
Yes, I thought I was better than all of you, but I've broken down
and am a sick animal. Sometimes, everyone in New York must need
to just go to the shops downstairs from their apartments, the kingdoms
they survey, and ask whoever is in there, whatever they sell, finally,
to breakdown and say, I have watched a thousand people come to you,
and now I am here. I am asking what you have. Help me.
This is your chance. I have come downstairs. I am asking for help.

History

Even Eve, the only soul in all of time
to never have to wait for love,
must have leaned some sleepless nights
alone against the garden wall
and wailed, cold, stupefied, and wild
and wished to trade-in all of Eden
to have but been a child.

In fact, I gather that is why she leapt and fell from grace,
that she might have a story of herself to tell
in some other place.

How to Go Home

You've got to go all the way around the earth
in order to get back to those people:
the luminous moon over a bassinet,
the great shoe widening out to a leg, the endless
torso, the lecturing head.

You've got to never go back home
but always go home forward,
ending every day further onward,
away from the good china,
away from your carpeted room.

Out there, on your way around the earth: true
love appeals to your sense of destination
but does not show up, oddly does not come
true. You've read that the Neanderthals,
according to the DNA, were not supplanted

but rather mated with the Sapien Sapiens
and you and I are the mix. It seems
this matter of worrying over with whom to sleep
extends backward a good long while,
and so little progress! Meanwhile,

you've got to get around the earth.
Or some other assignment. It's not altogether
arbitrary. You've got to perambulate a lot, that's
for certain, and you've got to come at the origins
of species from an unheard of direction: step out

into the first kitchen of your consciousness
from inside the squat refrigerator, or come up
from the drain in the sink. Or walk up to that man
in the backyard after having walked away from him
down and around the Earth.

And he still barbecuing! It's unbelievable.
Sure, the Neanderthals must have mooned
a good bit at the way things turned out,
the brooding brow, the pouting jaw, the pollen
in the grave. But you've still got to get out of there.

They were overtaken, yes, but that's a risk everyone
takes when they mate. That has to apply
to the women in the Capri pants spoon-feeding you
strained peas and the guy pausing between setting down
his briefcase and putting a key in your door.

It's not actually surprising that they wanted sleep so much
they knocked your chatterbox around.
Ah, well, go in circles around your violent memories.
It isn't utterly capricious that atoms and planetary systems
are both described by spinning one fist around the other.

The secret is apparently in the process of revolution,
around the earth and up the cellar stairs to some
original vision, to some platonic linoleum glare
in which truth might be found. And yet you keep just
going up the path. As if that could get you anywhere.

Breaking My Twenty

What are years for? No
one knows. Pockets where
our lost things go.

Somewhere below the pipelines,
below the school-yard,
below the chance of swinging higher,
below the feet of the dogs, the sod,
under the manhole,
somewhere under the rainfall, skies are blue
and the dreams that you dare to dream: what are years for?
No one knows; pockets where our lost things go.

Tilt down the brim of your hat and walk with me a moment.
Serious men have serious business. I want your
expertise. I want your sense of this matter. I have asked the others,
but it is over their heads.

Confidentially, this is what I want to show you:
this little bleeding thing.
A bloody muscle pumping at the center of the text.
Look here, this is the lower part that pulses, my battery
that hums, a moan. What's next? The stroke of midnight.
This is a shooting star
in the dome of the dark.

This is my heart.

If I were a bell I'd swallow my clacker.
That is the that in what is the matter.
If I were a hand I would pull off my fingers.
If I were your mouth. If I were a bell
I'd go ding-dong ding. Do you see what I mean?
This, apparently, is what you get from sex.
Come over here.

This, apparently, is the clatter of a greeting.
Look, let me just cut out my heart

and hand it over. You could look it over; tell me
what you think. Where are you going?

Take a few steps and talk to me a moment. They can wait.

What I want to say is that, in sum,
a lot of people think about the operation
after a certain amount of time passes and they might
do it if it weren't so expensive,
or if they thought the effect would last,
or be convincing.
What if the operation turned out
unpersuasive?

What if people walked away from you on the street
or in the supermarket saying to themselves,
Regarding the operation,
I remain unpersuaded.

What if your body, in turn, rejected your heart?
Down behind what the dog used to dig under,
below where he now disintegrates
is what our lovely volunteer was meant to be.

One day, long after the barbarians had lost interest in me,
I noticed something moving in the yard.
When you see yourself out there, digging, you are ashamed;
you consider the indignity of the flesh
and our post-Edenic trouble with the body comes to mind.
Don't worry, this time
I won't eat anything forbidden, I'm just tired and want
very much to sleep.

I want to be wherever there is nothing hidden underground,
no treasure and no bones, no buried lovers, no infant skulls,
no mastodons, no veils.

Let's have a hand for our lovely volunteer.
That's enough. Now get her a shovel.

It wasn't exactly your body they found, but it was
a body you remembered.
I'd like to wake up and blame myself for everything
so I could forgive the rest of you
your bodies; your bumper-car behinds.

Lips that are for kissing. Hands that are to bear.
What use pretending: cut I do bleed.

When I asked myself for my best advice she said: *Where are*
the papers? What is this bruise? We are only smoke and nerve,
eyes closed, cold sweat and self-accused. I'm sorry
it was such a mess. It took a terrible
long walk all the way west
before I guessed: the map had been misused.
Look at these place names I have abused! So cruel:
the skewed rule. Here is my swimming school
news: If you are on foot towards Autumn,
don't follow the tracks on the floor of the pool.

Then she disappeared and I got back to business.

All of this happened underneath where I know
what years are for.

Do you think I'm better off? You do.
(I'll have the boys bring your car around.)
Basement windows. Sewer grates. Pockets where
our lost things go.
I know a young lady who swallowed her life,
I don't know how.
What's the first thing you think of when you need to turn
yourself on? Don't whisper it. We're all indifferent.
Ollie ollie oxen free.

Our lovely volunteer is still digging, so we might
as well lean back and have a cold one.
I don't know why.
Then there was a thud:

shovel on wood,
shovel on metal.
And up came the box.

Then the dream of a blue cloudy sky.

.

So You're a Little Mentally Ill

Someone tells you something it's bad for you to know.
Where the body's buried for example.
Trouble's in you, after all this time.
Put there and ineradicable.
You move your eyes theatrically, back and forth,
trying to get to know fear by aping it.

One day a woman calls you on the phone,
you can hear the suit she's wearing,
and brings you over your two twin sisters,
long lost, sorry you never knew;
adoption, mix up at the hospital, Jackie
in Memphis, Maureen in Brooklyn, ten minutes
away all this time.
Jackie says let's all just sit in front of a mirror
for a minute. Maureen says call me Mo
and kisses your mouth using your own lips.
Charleston. Come on girls. Lindy Hop.

The girl in question is a virgin.

Worship with wet hands.
Submerge yourself in water and sing.

This is something that you can not control.
This is something that can not be denied.
Car crash. The presentation of a child
you had not meant to father.
That was when I saw the transparent man, Your Honor.
I wish I had not seen him but I did.
So these are my attributes. So this is my story.
So suddenly you realized
you would never fly in a plane again.

The girl in question is not a virgin anymore.
So you're a little mentally ill. So I'm unmarried.
So your wife turns out to be

a kleptomaniac. So your kid turns out to be
an Olympic swimmer. We were
the unmarked audience. Now we have interesting lives.

At Some Point Out

At some point out a life exceeds the speed
at which it can be easily directed.

That a life's intention somehow leaves the body,
at some age, and takes off go-cartishly, downhill.

There, these white rabbits come to look familiar
as the speed of light exceeds the speed of sound.

Among this rubble is the secret to your sexual
success, and yet the apartment keeps filling up.

At some age, the direction of a life is like a bone,
and intention is, for all its flexing, just a muscle.

Intention is just a muscle, tensing and releasing;
yet the secret to your sexual success is your voice.

The apartment is full of books and music over
which your voice is extremely hard to hear.

Enter the waistcoated rabbit, worried
that he's late. Familiar enough, but still disturbing.

The rushing suggests a destination and yet there is none,
beyond the rough patrician bedding of your voice.

With age we learn to judge a book by its cover: the part
we touch, what we see when we are not making use of it.

Intention, for all its flexing, is just a muscle; voice
the life intended, a shape of words beneath the one at hand.

The space between voice and body dies in bed and is
resurrected, as the speed of light exceeds the speed of sound.

At length, the synapse overtakes the nerve in its importance,
and your life exceeds its friction with the ground.

September

Tonight there must be people who are getting what they want.
I let my oars fall into the water.
Good for them. Good for them, getting what they want.

The night is so still that I forget to breathe.
The dark air is getting colder. Birds are leaving.

Tonight there are people getting just what they need.

The air is so still that it seems to stop my heart.
I remember you in a black and white photograph
taken this time of some year. You were leaning against a half-shed tree,
standing in the leaves the tree had lost.

When I finally exhale it takes forever to be over.

Tonight, there are people who are so happy,
that they have forgotten to worry about tomorrow.

Somewhere, people have entirely forgotten about tomorrow.
My hand trails in the water.
I should not have dropped those oars. Such a soft wind.

Please Answer All Three of the Following Essay Questions.

I

What would it take to make you
what you truly want to be and why will no one
cooperate with you on these visions you have
of yourself, when it would be so easy for them
to finally acknowledge that you are the demon
ruler of this island world and that all we eat
here is pickled herring that we harvest
from sycamore trees in the plenitude
of summer and load into mason jars for the lean
months of the cold? Do these men and women,
your subjects, fear you more than they love you?
What is it that they fear? Use a logical
proof; show your work.

II

If someone wanted to make you
slap them, hard, would it be better for him or
her to say that your father didn't like to hear you
sing, or to say that your mother purposefully pricked
her finger and bled into the coleslaw she brought
to the physics department picnics every year
because, despite her smile and gala disposition,
she had no taste for any of it, not for your father,
nor for you, nor for the logic of time and space
so she made them drink her sorrow
with their cabbage? Explain your answer.
Are you aware you can not save anyone from dying?

III

Why do you waste so much time considering
the juxtaposition of the perceived endlessness
of a moment and the micro-elapsement of a year?
Clearly there is nothing you can do about it and yet,

overcome with love for your friends and family
you neither run to them constantly and weep for them,
kissing their cast-off running shoes like a minor apostle,
nor do you refuse to answer the question "how are you"
ever again, certain that you don't know what it means.
By now you must recognize that rational
truth is unbearable and impossible to live by
and that everything possible and bearable is,
of necessity, a logical mess incorporating lies as well
as contradictory truths. And yet you just go along, making phone calls,
hanging curtains, letting the slanting sun before twilight
shift your thoughts,
riding the subway, sweeping the hallway,
and you watch TV, don't you, and go to the bank, eat
ice cream, call the cable guy, why do you do it
when you are so keenly aware of the impossibility
of your goals given the obdurate
resistance of such material? Try
to answer as completely as possible; time.

Waiting to Happen

The bottom of the town might open up
or influenza. Or everybody on the planet
finds a lump. Some man might plan
even now some foreign words to live
in the future's memory--as Kristallnacht
takes up space in ours. Saint
Bartholomew's Day Massacre. Bubonic
Plague. Consider now the length
of good times we've indulged in,
consider the bliss of sullen bus rides,
the paradise of trouble on the job,
the incommensurable dream of sexual
frustration, the joy of being mad and unfulfilled,
the glory of a night alone, lonely,
watching sitcoms; left out of the world.

On the other hand, this may be remembered
as the dawn of the golden age, wherein
after six millennia of disaster followed
on disaster, forever after no disaster comes.
Then this loneliness will never be redeemed.
If we never starve this bread will never seem
in hindsight to have been a feast of pleasure
is part of what I mean. But look at the books.
Consider the odds. We will very likely starve.

Stats

In any given year (as if I could give a year),
seven men in a town of ten thousand
will cry alone at home forty-two times.
That is the probability of that.

I don't know how many of them will cry thirty times.
It's not on the chart. It may be four,
or eleven. I am not at all sure
it would be any at all. Things fall through.

It is possible that thirty is a blip on the map.
Let's stick to that. Let's say that in a town
of ten thousand, not a single man will
cry alone at home thirty times. Rules break.

Damn the statistics. Let's spare them that, despite
the fact that forty of them will cry seven times.
Let's just insist that some number of men
do not sit down on the floor of their bathrooms,

poke at the dirt in the cracks of the tile, thirty times,
force a meaningful look to the ceiling,
lean hot sorrow heads to the cool bathtub lip,
go silent and choke and then cry.

As if a year were not a thing in which eleven
men weep thirty times alone up in their homes.
They don't. I say they don't. The world floats by.
What is the probability of that? Why.

Exodus

Millennia mount up and are we born older, each of us?
Layering the narratives and styles, do we age?
Here is the taut muscle of memory, it jerks and flexes in our sleep.
Awakened, we are the empty theater, the barren-bellied stage. Echoes
thunder inside us. There have been cataclysms, children, and storms
without rain. Of its own magnetic will, the pen avoids its page. (Even the
name avoids its thing.) Put your ear to me. What do you hear?

Remember: grave robbers came and stole our bracelets,
silver miners came and stole our grandfather's rings.
They took them off his fingers.
We stay quiet when we sing, avoid the unseen hand,
practice shibboleths in the foreign land, and drive all night through fields
of wheat and corn (so grain
remains the same?). Are we born older, each of us?
Here is the Nile, just as we left it. Here are the books, boiled in war.
Here are the fields we strode towards exile. We saw strong, shy faces,
signifying farms. (Walk on.)

The atmosphere is up there burning meteorites away.
Tremendous trees, above our heads, bear rain storms
and we, so small to them, and sheltered, keep moving;
migrating from nightingales to larks, from death to life,
and ever on from darkness into day,
and back through dark. (Why is it sacred?)
Because it is that way.

Gods and Animals

Call it solitude. Only gods and animals,
Aristotle said, can live alone. Nietzsche chided:
Also philosophers, who are a bit of each. Of course,
these days you root around a lot, bestial from the lack
of being seen. You look out of the windows
with wide, immortal eyes. But this is still

humanity, I think. Why let it end? Loneliness
for one, but what is that: The lack of a mood
swung at you; the lack of a common tongue?
Six of one. The *works cited* list is often better
than the text. Oh yes, the bliss of a common
fate. Yet what is fate nowadays, but familial

role: that from which one tries to break away,
and fails. Why bring in players, recreate it all at home?
The oracle sends you into therapy in hope you might
avoid the written word. But how far do you really think
you're getting? You animal. You god. Arrange
your bedding. The police are at the door.

Put away your pornographic coasters;
let their drinks make condensation rings.
So these are the decisions you are making?
The gods sleep all day. The animal eats
anything, the animal sleeps all day, emerging
in the night. Aristotle also sleeps all day,

but he is under stars who have souls. The nights
are bold soliloquy. The nights are oil paint
and ink. Having lost something, loneliness picks
through its garbage with a barge pole, unwilling
to get too close. So these are the decisions
I am making? (Fate might at any moment bring human

voices to your window. Fate might lift the roof
and move your solitude aside with a weird and human
joy.) Call it gratitude, I like to be alive
here in this railroad apartment hovering over
eternity. Here, you ride your whim. You can flex
your lecture. Here you can bark at your stars.

On the Strength of All Conviction and the Stamina of Love

Sometimes I think
we could have gone on.
All of us. Trying. Forever.

But they didn't fill
the desert with pyramids.
They just built some. Some.

They're not still out there,
building them now. Everyone,
everywhere, gets up, and goes home.

Yet we must not
diabolize time. Right?
We must not curse the passage of time.

III

No, I Would Not Leave You If You Suddenly Found God.

Praise wild dancing in the kitchen.
Praise sitting and talking to the doctor.
Praise phone calls from my sister.
Praise phone calls from you, a little drunk, leaning toward me.
Praise old lovers who show up when they are needed.
Praise our mothers, safe in another state.
Praise my apartment with its three wide rooms.
Praise the blue sky above the brick buildings.
Praise my back windows: trees, fire escapes, café lights.
Praise coffee (it destroys sadness).
Praise encyclopedias.
Praise you calling crying.
Praise ibuprofen.
Praise painting on wood.
Praise all the days in the photographs.
Praise the press of my breasts against the inside of my winter coat.
Praise the name of my winter coat: Big Black.
Praise this feeling of trying to write about the truth.
Praise the Byzantine Empire.
Praise the salt in sweat. We are not alone. Praise making you laugh.
Praise making you proud.
Praise the second cup of coffee.
Praise having a party to go to tonight.
Praise my halting therapist.
Praise mixed baby lettuce.
Praise my confidence.
Praise my talent.
Praise bravery in the face of fear.
Praise my fearlessness.
Praise my fear.
Praise pickled herring with onions.
Praise the Arctic Circle.
Praise the Mighty Tonka truck.
Praise the forklift; praise the crane.
Praise theater tickets.
Praise the repetition of names.
Praise the Virgin.

Praise the Magdalene.
Praise Magellan.
Praise Central Park.
Praise your uneven teeth.
Praise blood-stained sheets.
Praise the land, and what I know about its bedrock.
Praise David, dancing wild around the ark of his Lord.
Praise the job of work of truth.
Praise the phrase "job of work."
Praise your faith in me.
Praise your courage.
Praise my faithfulness.
Praise my dedication.
Praise that you sleep with one eye open because a dog bit your face.
Praise your extra nipple.
Praise that we are not lovers.
Praise that we touch each other like lovers.
Praise that you figure out the movie before me.
Praise my desperation.
Praise my terrible fear.
Praise Jones Beach.
Praise the boys in long pants selling frozen Snickers at the sea shore.
Praise death.
Praise the memory of being tiny and tumbled under the ocean, close
to death. Praise arch support.
Praise chewing on a steak bone.
Praise other people's poems.
Praise the Empire State Building.
Praise swimming out so far, I forget the fact of land.
Praise eating chicken-cutlet sandwiches with my brother at the beach.
Praise doing the puzzle with my mother.
Praise my father explaining the universe.
Praise that after visiting Great-Grandma Bertha's,
we went to Coney Island.
Praise three of us fitting in one seat on the Cyclone.
Praise the weird little town where you were raised.
Praise that you were born here where I was born.
Praise the ex-lovers we have in common; praise chocolate.
Praise living at the millennium.
Praise the rotary phone.

Praise broccoli rabe with garlic and olive oil.
Praise total abandon.
Praise bringing out the harpies.
Praise using every muscle.
Praise thirst and water.
Praise the landing on the moon.
Praise singing loud and hard.
Praise going to bed exhausted.
Praise your poems.
Praise my poems.
Praise that we drink too much.
Praise you promising me that you will stop smoking.
Praise how I moon over you.
Praise how you love me.
Praise your strong husband.
Praise dancing to swing.
Praise dancing to the blues.
Praise the borscht at Veselka.
Praise my first gray hairs.
Praise acetaminophen.
Praise Australopithecus.
Praise speaking the truth.
Praise knowing that life is an endeavor of truth.
Praise knowing that life is the becoming towards truth.
Praise the authentic moments of working with someone towards truth.
Praise desire.
Praise stupefying desire.
Praise north and south.
Praise the yellow sun on the red brick buildings outside my windows.
Praise knowing that it is midnight out the back window
because the café lights go off.
Praise oranges.
Praise midnight out the front windows and the Empire State Building
goes dark.
Praise Cézanne's apples and oranges.
Praise men from their callused feet to their beautiful thinning hair.
Praise women from Sappho biting her lip
through the first hip-swagger of the new millennium.
Praise the shark giving birth to live young.
Praise the bird.

Praise that I can not stop making this list.
Praise the pleasure of making this list.
Praise whatever will finally stop my making this list.
Praise drinking with you and talking poetry and sex.
Praise that I tell you everything.
Praise that honesty is terrifying.
Praise my students.
Praise my beautiful, curious, deferential students.
Praise that neither you nor I have ever been more than
passingly brutalized.
Praise humility in the face of love.
Praise submission to the truth.
Praise the rituals of life on Earth.
Praise the candles and the incense and the chocolate coins.
Praise tiny Japanese statues dedicated to aborted children.
Praise feeding my sins to the ducks.
Praise coming of age.
Praise unplaced lines of poetry.
Praise the New York Times and Comedy Central.
Praise endless, tongueless kisses.
Praise the word "midriff."
Praise the dictionary.
Praise the way you say "scrub my teeth" instead of brush.
Praise that you lost your snake in your apartment
and found him ten months later.
Praise that I am not ashamed.
Praise your father's stark white hair.
Praise your mother, measuring our waists in the Washington Square
Hotel. Praise the clues about your birth mother.
Praise the hints about your birth father.
Praise that he was a professor and she a student at the University
where I got my degree. Praise my degree.
Praise you and your husband watching me graduate. Praise watching you
get married at City Hall and riding the subway home. Praise how
surprised I am that we have this love.
Praise bravery.
Praise dancing.
Praise suddenly knowing the right thing.
Praise running to do the right thing.
Praise running towards love.

Praise the words "decapitated" and "disembodied."
Praise rhyme.
Praise meter.
Praise certainty.
Praise indivisibility.
Praise the movies; praise writing songs.
Praise asking each other when we are supposed to bleed.
Praise talking to myself alone in the dark.
Praise my endless pleasure in the godless solitude of my private mind.
Praise the giraffe and the porcupine.
Praise sloth.
Praise gluttony.
Praise a man's hand pressing the small of my back.
Praise your tiny feet.
Praise travel.
Praise the refusal of travel.
Praise your blue eyes.
Praise kissing men: desert of whiskers, oasis of lips.
Praise kissing women and the effort not to bite.
Praise the lips and the tongues and the grease.
Praise the feast.
Praise agony.
Praise defeat.
Praise that we used to dance in public and that now we dance at home.
Praise faith.
Praise glory.
Praise praise.
Praise your brilliant heart.
Praise the mystical abundance of your horrifying heart.
No, I will not leave you if you want to worship God.

Tiger Story

I used to mangle around the jungle;
stalk things, tail up in the high grass
brazen, stripéd, cruel.
Smelling the grazing bison one night,
hungry,
I made a nice move, breathing the wet fur
of a herd, tracing a path behind this wall of grass
past which the antelope
can not see, and then coming out
full speed, bounding, hard land coming up
under my feet and then plummeting
away again, my heart beating in
my paws, my claws pulsing,
engorged. And I'm seeing the end
of the wall of grass, and as I
turn toward the lake, they all see
and smell and hear me
all at once, frozen time, their frozen
fear of me, but I am still moving,
aware, but flying through the
frozen moment, above it, in the
desert air and then, then they turn
and run. They make a noise
and the stink of their fear fills the world
and I dive into it, towards the lake where
I know, as I know the taste of my teeth:
there are some young ones in there,
deep in the lake, neck deep, no way
they can run in that
as fast as I can leap.
The endless herd turned tail
and ran and I, aloft on the smell of them,
aloft on the cloud of their white,
upright tails, I saw her, a little doe
and knew her, and flew into the air above
the lake and came down as she looked
up at me as if I were a bird

and not the clawed muscle of death
descending and I let my right front paw down first,
slitting her small throat with my fore-claw
and digging in so my body swung around
her neck and I opened my mouth and leading
with my tongue, tasting her fur, then my teeth;
I bore down with a flick of my jaw and broke
her neck. Easy there, stay calm, I say
to myself, because I am still in the water, it would
be over my head if I stood so I am swimming
with my kill in my mouth and the blood is starting
to swell and the deep thick stench of it
going up my nose and making me sick
with hunger, my hair on end,
and my flesh breaks out in a sweat
from above my eyes to my haunches
and the hot oily sweat beads up under the cold
lake water, I'm salivating, I've got to get to the shore
soon, kill still twitching, stampede of feet
still pounding all around me, and through it
that noise of one mournful moan and I swim
through it, all the way to the shore,
the mother moan, honing me in to the shore
and then she looks at me and
knows and shows nothing and turns her
tail at me and runs, into the tall grass, crazy, away
from me, the end of the world, the end of her season.
On land I paused and breathed the twilight air
then dragged it up until I couldn't wait
and licked the kill's wound and tore it
open, the luxury of that, always bizarre,
no other cubs coming for it, no sharing
a gift from a mother, just mine, the whole
of it my kill, my hot, bleeding, abundant kill.
I slit it with my teeth and the gut falls out
and I lick at it and go for the upper front leg
and rip off a mouthful at once, the baby fat
of it dripping down my face, into my throat
and I eat and I eat, drunk, talented, obscene.

I was guarding my kill, lying near it
stuffed but worried, the thing, if I could keep it,
would feed me for five days at the least --
maybe a week. Usually I'd drag it somewhere
high, but here there are no trees I could climb
and otherwise usually I would cover it by turning round
and flipping dead, tall grass back behind me, over the kill,
but here, there's nothing but rocks and they will
not pile like grass nor keep out the smell
of my kill. Sweet kill. Only half a leg
and the offal gone. Face still there, tongue out
between your teeth. As a cub I loved to eat that
first, mostly because there was no competition
for it, but also because it was fun to touch tongues;
to eat a face. But I was young.
I reminisced like this, awake but thick-headed from my
feast and then I fell asleep
beside it. And then I was awake.
There was a noise, far off and then near,
and then he was there, in front of me in the early
dawn light, this tremendous male
his tail flicking the air and I knew as I always
knew, the dawn was his, he was too big,
he would take my week of food, my kill.
Normally, I would have walked away a bit,
giving it up, but staying near, lingering,
watching him lick my kill.
This time was different I suppose because he
didn't even try, he was so huge, he didn't
make a noise or show a paw, he just came on
and almost, I thought,
smirked and I looked into the eyes of my kill
and back at his and smelled the start of sweet
rot on my kill and smelled the male's self-certain musk
and then I rushed him,
wailed toward him,
defending, for the first time in my life,
my kill against a huge male tiger, a tiger
who could surely take my life.
He did not take my life, he merely flayed my thigh.

A big hunk of thick skin was hanging off.
I was bleeding and had not even tried
to swing at him yet, I was diving for him when he reared
and swatted a hunk of me right off of me
and I lost consciousness for a fleet second and when
I arose he was looking at me as I look at things
when I have left them half-dead and I
crawled off into the high grass,
very wounded. Light-headed. Scared.
The next day came and went, I hadn't moved
much: around in circles near the lake,
thirsty and weak all the time. Weaker
every moment. Thirsty again at every
breeze. Then I felt a hard blow
to my shoulder and fell asleep.

When I woke up, I was in a white world.
The world was gone. There was nothing
beneath or above or around me, nothing
smelled of anything and nothing felt of anything
and nothing tasted. I saw nothing but white
and the faint smell of monkey mixed with
sweet smells and pain.
The whole world was gone. I supposed
that this was the next part of life,
the white-walled, skyless stage of life
with white robed figures moving
beyond reach. I slept, I wondered where
I was and where the jungle was and how long
white walls would be the world.
Was I still on earth? I slept, I ate someone
else's kill. I drank strange waters. I licked
at my wound, but my wound was gone,
the hunk of me that was hanging off of me
was back on me, though swollen and hairless,
and red. Sometimes, in that life, I would feel another
blow and fall out of myself and wake up
later, with a new taste to my wound.

And then one day I woke up moving, without
moving, the world was back, but I was not in it.
I was in a small white room that was moving
through the world and then the room opened
and I waited, and looked out into the world of grass
and sky and sprang out of the room, my haunch
as good as new and the good season was still
with us and I was strong from the steady food
of the white world and ready to live.

I sauntered into my tall grasses feeling the earth
give way under my feet and the insects flocking
towards me and the sun on my back
and the world of smells, dead, living, rotting flesh,
fresh kills, newborns, old toothless beasts,
bodies everywhere again, wide open world.

Years passed by, monsoon, cold drought
hot drought, monsoon, cubs have come and gone
dear things, looking like me, learning to fight
and moving on, and I have taken to lying sometimes
in a shallow lake, where all the antelope can see me
and staying there, so peacefully, so long
that they get used to me, and drink at the edges
of my lake. I don't know. I used to mangle
around the plains, you would see me everywhere
at once. I have outlived those with whom I was
a cub, I have killed only what I need to eat.
I have even enjoyed hunger. Food always comes
before I grow weak. I like to lie in my lake
and think about the white room and wonder if I
will go back there, and wonder if I ever was there,
and wonder if everyone goes there sometimes.
Cool room. Strange water. Strange sleep.

Totem and Taboo

You can only go up the attic stairs and only go down

the basement. You hide in the well of the gap of dark made by the arch
of the back of the couch. You crawl out onto the roof at night

and smoke cigarettes. Your father didn't like jewelry; his wedding ring

rested on his shelf of things. Above you a hieroglyph of hats
nest each other in difficult clusters. Drawers are filled with beads.

Beads are not for prayer but somehow suggest it. Drawers

are filled with socks; drawers are filled with cotton
shirts; drawers are filled with silks and straps,

with hook and eye contraptions. In his closet is a pipe,

a collection of silver dollars, a passport, and a gun.
With your eyes closed: Go to where your father kept his gun

when you were young. Open the door to it and take it down.

Wave it around. Act reckless with it, this is only a dream.
Prove to yourself that this is a dream: point the gun

at your head and pull the trigger. You are still here,

reading this in your chair. Take the pipe and the gun
and the silver dollars. Go to the shelf of his things and take his ring.

Go to her jewelry drawer and string the pearls around your neck.

Take the earrings that you were not allowed to touch and place them
in a careless pocket. Cover yourself in the relics

and the sacred of your childhood, slop them all over

yourself, giddy-eyed, his favorite tie, her wedding veil
in your back pocket, and go down to the basement, laden,

leave the lights off, twirling the gun, tread on the veil,

dare the monsters, sit down on the floor, not singing,
don't speak. Sit alone in the dark in that cavern of fear

and breathe its basement air. Much later, when you are

familiar, when you have handled
the gun and the pipe and the silks and the pearls and known them

as casual things made of ore and wood and worms and mollusks

and not the untouchable totemic centers of the world,
carry your burden up the attic stairs, your head tilted

toward the moonlight from the window up there,

walk out onto the roof of the house that you lived in,
the town around you rising and falling like a sleeping body,

saunter un-cautiously to the chimney and down it drop

all those things, silver dollars, silken bands, the ring. Then with one step
off the roof, over the town of asphalt and stone, land back in your chair.

Put down the book and look at your hands. Look at the wall.

IV

Sailing with Virgins

I

As luck would have it, the angels missed the girl
and so she never knew. Years
milling about the stables,
restless, wielding pitchforks at the grain.
Then, from a distance, news of the English routed
and the whole thing over. Other angels loiter
on their route and a girl lathes away
her years in a carpenter's room.
Then one day: it's the apotheosis and she sees
she's missed the gist
of her narrative.
Bye, kid. I wish I'd known.
It is a matter of that,
a moment, a casual compunction
to drink light coffee tepid or black coffee hot,
and you either miss or receive your connection.
And there's the proverbial boat,
and me on it! I seem
to be talking to someone; someone large,
yet ethereal. I can not brace myself
without help. I list towards the stern
of myself and bend the boat's bow. Oh well.
With or without luck, the heart bangs around
on its bed. The belly grumbles.

II

Those virgins that I mentioned did, of course,
get the news. At first, both were just grateful
to now have something else to lose, but to whom
can you confide such information? Worse,
who would understand? It must have been lonely:
chosen, but not yet showing. I'd like to be
with them; Joan barely post-pubescent, taking her
sword with her even to bed, and Mary drowsing

through her first trimester, beatific,
both leaning on the poet's arms. Mary in drapes,
Joan in armor, me in a t-shirt and tan cotton pants.
And all on a boat, as I said, sailing. Lucky, I guess,
to have caught it. Mary demurs praise, citing
her parents' support, Joan speaks mildly
of unsympathetic folk and chalks
our party up to luck. Mary says *No, that large archangel*
saw you had the right stuff. Joan says, *Still,*
dumb luck to have it. Supportive or not, advice
from elders, is, for us, as much a sliver in the distance
as is the land—and the land is almost gone.
Clouds gather. A flock of gray birds shaped like arrows
floats just overhead, but no one points and no one
names them. These girls have taut and gentle
skin, they flex and tire, readying to make the myriad
decisions that alone will bring the mythic vision
into being; chosen, but not yet showing. The sense of portent
is overwhelming on some nights,
in the dark sea air, but mostly it's just day-to-day.
They have such familiar faces. Such similar shapes;
soft-red mouths and sweet, predictive tongues.
Both frown a bit even when they
smile. Joan speaks little but says that she'll
die young. Mary shrugs that Yes, so will her son.
I've got the railing. The land is gone. So this is luck.

Convince Him

Alexander couldn't

sweet talk his men into sacking one more city,
so he leapt over the wall; what could they do

but follow? His father knew what his son was

in some ways but not in others;
he never found out what he did, out

there, to always win. Other fathers wonder, too,

still self-assured, yet somehow ill at ease
with so many strategies in use these days;

so many other children's efforts underway.

Sometimes you build cities, sometimes you just
give them your name. You have to have

a sense of timing with a thing like this,

and you have to be more brutal than your father.
When planning cities, consider how it would feel

to roam around their streets after you are dead

and all alone. No wonder Alexander talked to him
most often when he wasn't in the room,

saving all the stronger stories for the pyre-talk

and the ghost. Out there, these days, young conquering
ghosts still run naked along the taxicabs to show

the passengers that they love them; that they

will not be abandoned if it all comes down. Even now
there is the danger that it may yet all come down.

Despite our boundless luck, there is a chance

that some soon campaign will be disastrous
and our own city sacked: walls kneeling and windows

popping out of their International Style frames,

the Lever House and the Seagram Building clattering,
while subways threaten to plow up

through the earth like sea monsters

yet nothing moves. What would he have
done in the face of such resilience? Nothing moves

all night long: arms, legs, everything stiff

to the empty room, unmoving, in attendance,
up. And nothing coming over the wall

to lay siege to me or up

from under the world to crown
against my name. What could such solitude

lead to if not strategy? If not the exercise

of muscles otherwise unused? Conquering suddenly
comes easy, plunder falls into place. And who could fix blame,

with so much of the world still not Macedonian? What

do these ghosts of fathers want,
an explanation? Would they want to know

what goes on out there; the leaping, the abandonment

to the darkness on the other side
of one wall and another? Talk to the smoke.

Tell your story to the shift in the afternoon light.

Speak openly to the light. Call it father. Explain
that you grew up, and that now you own the world.

Love Sonnet on the Progress of the Soul

Well hell's bells, here are the hands to rub me from my weather.
A voice inhales as wooden stairwells drop me from my day.
Will it go on this way? This is a swing from tether to no tether,
it widens into the open wind, it vines into the sky and leaps away.
Do we will it to go on that way? Heavens to Betsy, the bounty of all,
swell of a sandbar, turn of a tide, the wealth of coins and shoes;
Lured by such dancing even caryatids sometimes saunter off their wall.
I fall. This is the wide open ocean. This is what land-lovers lose.
Do we choose the hands to smudge our sand into the sea?
We do. The carnival tightrope act of sequined flesh and bone
and sweet knows when to leap. Light splatters through the leaves.
And me. Well hell's bells, the light careens against my stone.

A quiet kissing cloud begins to spread and hover over.
We tumble to a world of other weather.

Rapture

The two-tone girl, mouth wide open, head back,
squinting blind at the rock stars on stage. Screaming.

Louder than the music; so loud out here that
in her head it must have been astounding.

Above her, on the stage, the musicians keep playing.
They sway their elegant teenaged hips to music even they

can only feel. Outside, geese fly overhead, honking.
Dogs listen with their bodies and then bark.

Wings bat at the ancient night air so that it rushes
like love out of breath beneath the flock.

A man says *listen* and stretches his neck to do it.
A woman says *listen* and covers her eyes with her hands.

Insomnia

Possession of knowledge, casual as sleep,
is as tormented, and no easier to keep
in days as silent as imagined sabbaths
of dissipated, swallowed rage
and nights as loud as footsteps
in the lizard age.

My mind is mattered, like Darwin's tree, felled
with causal laws, and beast of earth and sea
where notions splinter as white roots spread, unheld;
expatriated three months deep
I sit up in my Paris bed
and I can not sleep.

In sleeplessness, which trembles clarity,
gestures grow, in operatic parody:
kimonoed in a blanket at quarter after three
I slowly swallow small white drugs
and drink my water like pale tea
from an earthen mug.

While in other houses, faces slack and snore
like dancing braggart spirits, safely on the other shore,
I re-mumble the words of my pharmacist,
who shivered like a frightened wren:
Voilà Madame, and checked her wrist,
Vous allez dormir bien.
Possessing the package, I read with some alarm:
contents listed belladonna,
which I thought did only harm.

On the phone my friend explained the potion
as a homeopathic notion:
put a little poison in and kill what's eerie
in the blood and bones.
But even sleeping pills? I queried.
She shrugged the telephone.

Now as I hover waiting for an artificial drowse
I haze to think the metaphor
that in me lurks there something bad
for my nocturnal wakefulness
is better than the one I had
which spoke of stress, which if pressed, I must admit
I do not know what is.

I know far less who is this dour belladonna.
Encyclopedias at the Sorbonne
say it has a purple flower
and pretty roots that can give you sleepy eyes
if you do not take enough to die.
Italian women used its round black berry
to make their eyes shine like drops of rain
(though I can't imagine how)
and hence its name.

It seemed to me I could not sleep
because I thought too many things:
difference between strong and weak forces,
where to find archival sources
on the rights of kings,
how to move my knight just right
when bishops call it pinned,
and how to fly a flagging life
in just a breath of wind.

There were conjectures, too, and questions.
Perhaps Czar Nicholas escaped,
or did he die there in the pit?
Perhaps Lolita loved Humbert
if just a little bit.
Did Anna think of music,
there waiting on the tracks, inert?
When Jude's Sue leapt from the window
how was she not then hurt?

Maybe genes are egoist
when they make their tiny bid;
maybe Jacob never lied; and
maybe Desdemona did.

Do wordless beasts complain of heartache?
Even silent fish may moan and fill
unfathomable deep darkness
with the coos of groaning gills.
It all crashed raucous in my mind.
Proof dinosaurs are not yet dead:
they lope the night inside my head,
with meteors behind.

What do hard fast sleepers know
of spiral stairwells in the night,
those who in the first declension of the day
can but repeat their rubbled dreams from the tangle of their sheets
blinking pennied, unfresh eyes like Lazarus alive
with nothing more to tell of than the terror of the blind?
For them the night is never more
than a distant, scrambled memoir
from another country's war.

With time to think, we do not think
but settle into time, as water settles into sand.
But press the brash unwilling mind, if just
to trust, if just to sleep,
and it will snort and filibust and dig its caverns deep.

Knowledge batters love and duty,
it runs like terror beasts unkept;
then like an inverse sleeping beauty
strange belladonna kissed me and I slept.

Telling the Future

I certainly would have thought we'd have those flight packs by now.
The mother sees a dead bird in the driveway and tells the children
the coincidence of dead-bird sightings
                    and phone calls announcing death.

Flag flies at half-mast. Bough breaks. There are two ways to get
around: elevated trains and undergrounders. There is no surface travel;
the only way to go is over your head or under your
                    skin. The next test will entail

a shift in perspective. Fire when ready. Shouldn't you put down
a towel? It's very messy. Embraceable you. That was when we realized
the cat was pregnant. Then suddenly, something goes wrong
                    and you have the time of your life.

I had expected by now we would have lived forever: sculpting the way we
feel about the others when they look down, and ever so slightly away, out
of alabaster, hearing the same untrustworthy voices, day
                    after day talking about vegetables,

and how my hair looks best, and which newscaster to believe. While other
animals hide to die, small birds do it on the sidewalk. As if
featherless resting in the moss cracks was a common
                    stage of life. Remember him?

Remember the equations? The sense of cause-effect? The expectation of
protection we each were welcome to believe? I would have thought by
now the picture-phone would be everywhere; and everyone
                    would see you when you speak.

Trotsky's Hand

I

It's like dreaming of someone
too much while you're away
at war; then you come home
to his fingered hat or her

faltering hemline and it's
What the hell was I fighting

for? Just another example
of how biography works.
Your character has got
to have a narrative arc,

some drawbacks,
something irredeemably awful,

along with his or her strong
points, to be believable.
Yet we all recoil in disbelief
when anything of the sort cuts

a form into our real lives,
the life of the author. Don't

despair! It's just the demands
of narrative! Leda, after all,
probably never even thought
to fear anything like *that*.

Then one day, there it is,
the century actually over

and most of its artifacts
still entirely inexplicable.
This is no walk in the park
with spinach, Swee'pea,

I've got no idea where to go
for extra strength.

I guess that's what
they're selling.
It's an incidental
that it cleans your laundry,

scrubs your teeth. What is of note
is that it is a source of extra

strength. Extra strength! Thank
God! That's what we're going
to need in case they all switch back:
the swan, the prince, the salt.

Even if you weren't ever accosted
by a feathery god,

you take some heavy losses early on,
and that will leave feathers everywhere
for the rest of your life; as if
you were wearing an eiderdown coat;

you just walk around and molt.
As for the man in the tiara,

that's a transformation
you never want to go through
twice, but do, coaxing every
so often your sad, damp, frog

back into his palace. *Don't
you like your scepter? Won't*

you wear your robes?
Lastly, salt. Well, who doesn't
turn towards the sepia for a second
look; into the carousel music

and the tortured plaster horses
of the past? But this sympathy

does not imply that I want
Madame Lot back here
knitting itchy sweaters.
Let's just try to calm down.

II

When Stalin took power
he had Trotsky erased
from the photographs.
Sometimes, you can still see

a floating hand. Left behind.
So disembodied as to be

almost meaningless. We try
to ignore it, floating there
in history. We get to work.
There is something to be said for that.

You can't really expect me
to roll around naked in a garden

letting Trotsky's severed hand
float around my body,
knowing my body better
than any lover, his soft,

soft-focused, probing hand.
Yet, how can we do anything

serious with that thing hovering
overhead? A woman working
at a table in the park swats
away the tickling hand

of Trotsky, and intones
as if to all of history:

Not now. Trotsky's hand,
abashed, moves on
to pick some flowers.
So much is gone that

what is left is inexplicable
without memory, and memory

is painful and very difficult
to explain. Which isn't
to say I mind Trotsky's hand

snapping its fingers
and flapping itself like a bird

above my desk or would rather
have him back, extant,
yammering about world socialism
and complaining about

the samovar: *Is this thing cold again?*
So, is this more of a lament

than a complaint? Sure.
But it is always there. This
burden of history is not a bird
but a hand, its wrist a tiny cloud.

It's very quiet. It fills the quiet sky.

Villanelle If You Want to Be a Bad-Ass

You will not be rewarded for remaining long the same.
You will, of course, be taunted if you ever try to change.
When trainers wander off, tigers, please do not stay tame.

Consistency is worse, it brings the wrong kind of fame.
The orbit of right action has a freakin' woolly range.
You will not be rewarded for remaining long the same.

It, inertia, is a pity. It, stagnation, is a shame. Yet you
yourself preach caution as you pace your unlocked cage:
"When trainers wander off, tigers, please do not. Stay tame."

Be a mountain if you want to, be the whole mountain range.
Will you, in turn, be hostage to your hostage on the page?
You will not. Be rewarded for remaining long the same?

You can say what you want when the angel makes you lame.
You can wrestle against water, you can rape your own rage
(when trainers wander off). Tigers, please do not stay tame.

As hard as bleeding a tree to death by cut and squeezing, change
from out of the gut of the rut's range will be insanely hard.
But you will not be rewarded for remaining long the same,
when trainers wander off, tigers, please do not stay tame.

Again with the Boxes

Guy comes out of the mosque,
white robed and a shmata on his head,
Eleventh Street, east side of Manhattan,
white moon plumping in a deep blue sky,
those painterly clouds going by slow;
he faces Mecca, lets out a call,
pauses, enthralled, like all of us,
with the sky and the newness
of autumn, the crisp chill.

Then the guy goes down these stairs
to where someone is always leaving
cardboard boxes, maybe it's the mosque
that leaves them, he pads over in his
fancy slippers, places the boxes
one inside another, tidying up,
then up the little stairs, waits;
then again bellows his call,
like a bruise on the night.

The milk-full moon lights his way back down,
where he adjusts again the cartons
that have fallen as he called.
I watch, guessing in his head he says:
Pray to Mecca, mess with the boxes,
pray to Mecca, mess with the boxes.
It all makes me feel like such a Jew,
the sigh of this big guy with a white
thingy on his head, Oy, so *again*
with the boxes I'm thinking. *Oh so*
them too, with the boxes and with
the praying and the shmata on your head.

And what are you gonna do? There it is,
up to you to do it, to turn and say what is
to be said, with the thing on your head,
and then to screw with the boxes outside your
mosque. Because that is what is right in front
of you. That is where the moon alights for you.

The Bottom of the Nile

Rowing in my bed towards water
I can not help but make my longing
be a sound. I swaddle it in cloth. I frown.

Expecting no one
like the pharaoh's listening daughter,
I shift the basket's weight
and let it drown.

The bottom of the Nile
is layered with the bones
of little unsaved Moseses,
or is it Mosesi? Sorrow, too,
which can not float,
goes there to die.

Swamp Thing

I

Apparently you've got to be
vulnerable if you want
anything to happen,
and on the other side of it
you've got to be unfathomably
strong in order to get by.
In order to get through the attacks
and rejections occasioned
by vulnerability you've got to
be almost invulnerably
strong. It's a difficult road map
to fold, friends. The shifts in logic
are very subtle, they have
to do with generational time
and we don't have that
kind of time lying around
in the storeroom, we've got
to get it on special order,
which means you've got to
read about a thousand books.

II

So, to review, the inner life
is lousy with affection
for the outer life which seems
like a sweet, dumb child
that has somehow survived
a week alone, lost in intemperate
circumstance, an actual swamp
in the bayou, and our inner life
wonders, how did that stupid
child I love so tenderly
and with so little outward show
of derision possibly survive out there
where the possibility of being eaten

by a crocodile is very real,
grabbed by snakes, being bitten by endless
mosquitoes, and drowned, let alone
freezing, let alone starved.

III

Survival experts opine
that your idiot outer life
survived in the Bayou
because it never thought
to panic, it never noticed
that it was time to give up.
Our inner life wonders
how this naïve assumption
of existence is communicated
to the crocodiles and the snakes
but the survival expert is gone:
wanted to be the first one
out of the parking lot, just
in case. I guess I understand.

IV

How did it ever get construed
that the child of us is inner? It's
the outer that always has to be told
to *Take that out of your mouth.*
I've got something twice as inner
that sits quietly writing her book.
Perhaps our outer self ate algae.
Bumble bumble, the deadline
for the grant is long past,
long past,
but some part of you writes
for guidelines. *I realize that the
deadline is past but I want to
express my desire to have applied.*
This is not what the survival
expert had in mind.

V

Staring out the window
towards First Avenue, the inner
self lectures. *Vulnerability,*
it explains to the outer self,
is a difficult mess. Yes, apply
for the grant but not when the deadline
is so long past. As for asking your lover
to move in, perhaps you remember
your stay in the swamp? The yellow
eyes of those who see when you
are nightly blinded? The legless
finesse of the serpents? The tug
of vines? Well, who am I to caution
your affections. By now the outer self
is on the phone, making the arrangements,
not particularly concerned; eager
for all of it. Hoping to win
grants for which it never applied
and sliding down some secret
handrail, open-armed, wide-eyed,
into the din of life. Apparently,
it is crazy in love, and reckless
with the customs of survival.